WHAT WOULD YOU BE?
in Ancient Greece

First published in Great Britain in 2024
by NQ Publishers, an imprint of Nextquisite Ltd.

Copyright © 2024 by Nextquisite Ltd

All rights reserved. Unauthorized reproduction,
in any manner, is prohibited.

www.nqpublishers.com
www.nextquisite.com

Project Director Anne McRae
Art Director Marco Nardi

Illustrations Steph Marshall
Text Mary Auld
Editing Rachel Cooke, Andrew Cornwell
Picture Research Nicola Burns
Graphic Design Marco Nardi

ISBN 978-1-912944-62-0

Printed in China

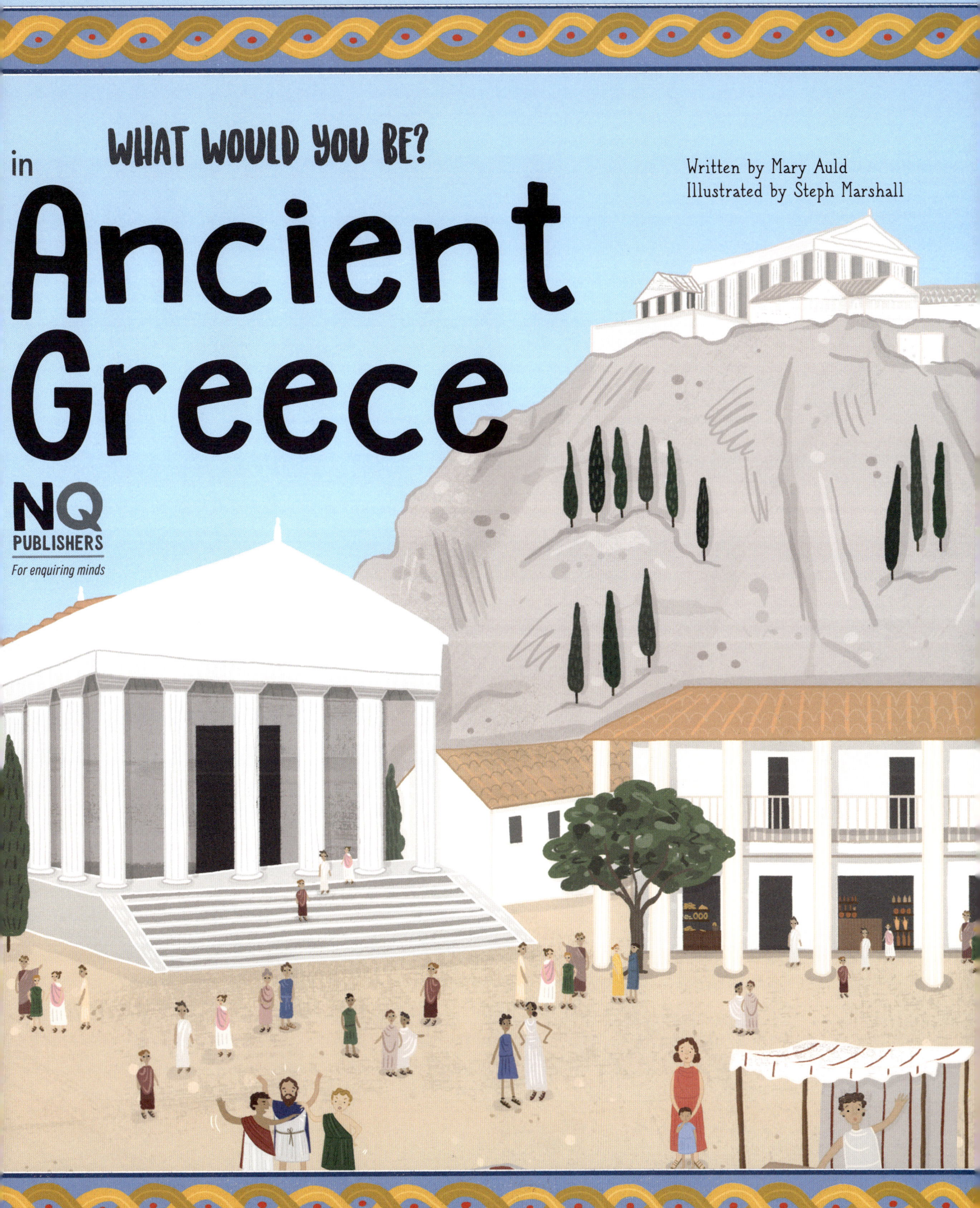

CONTENTS

LIVING IN ANCIENT GREECE   10
Timeline

THE YOUNG PRIESTESS   12
The Minoans

THE GREEK WORLD   14
Colonies and Trade

A FARMING FAMILY   16
Agriculture and Food

THE YOUNG BARD   18
Gods, Goddesses and Myths

THE HOPLITE   20
Soldiers, Wars and Weapons

THE OARSMAN   22
Greek Battleships

THE APPRENTICE POTTER   24
Pottery and Vase Painting

THE OLYMPICS   26
Sporting Events

THE FISHMONGER — 28
Living in a Greek City

THE CLUMSY CHORUS BOY — 30
Greek Theatre

A WOMAN DOCTOR — 32
Health and Medicine

LEON GOES TO SCHOOL — 34
Education and Learning

ZOE STAYS AT HOME — 36
Family Life

THE GOSSIPY BARBER'S SHOP — 38
City-States and Democracy

THE YOUNG PAINTER — 40
Art and Architecture

QUIZ TIME! — 42
INDEX — 44

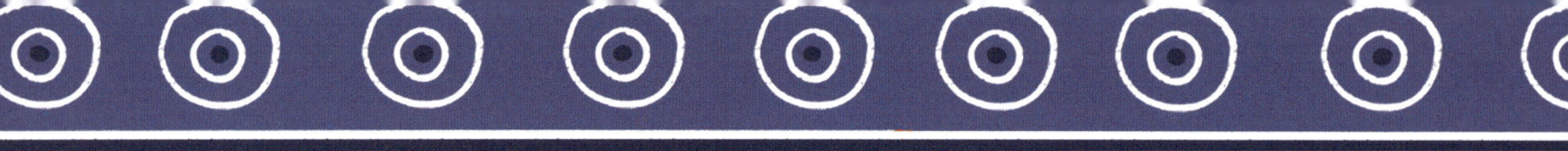

TIMELINE

Dates in this book are shown as BCE (Before Common Era) and CE (Common Era). The Common Era starts with year 1.

MINOAN TIMES
(3000–1100 BCE)
A Mediterranean civilisation centred on the island of Crete with strong links to the Greek mainland.

MYCENAEAN TIMES
(1700–1100 BCE)
The Mycenaeans create the first mainland Greek civilisation. They fight the Trojan Wars.

THE DARK AGES
(1100–800 BCE)
Mycenaean civilisation collapses and its writing system is forgotten.

THE ARCHAIC PERIOD
(800–480 BCE)
Greek city-states are formed and Greeks begin to set up colonies. A new Greek writing system develops.

THE CLASSICAL PERIOD
(479–323 BCE)
Although often at war, the Greeks develop many ideas that influence later Western thought.

THE HELLENISTIC PERIOD
(323–30 BCE)
Named for "Hellas", the ancient Greek for Greece. It ends when the Roman Empire is established.

1500 BCE
Minoan civilisation at its height
The Minoans rule Crete and their influence spreads to mainland Greece. Frescoes of bull jumping are painted at their main palace on Crete, Knossos.

1180 BCE
The end of the Trojan War
The city of Troy is destroyed, ending the Trojan War fought between the Mycenaeans and the Trojans.

c. 700 BCE
Greek farming described
A Greek poet, Hesiod, describes farming. About this time the Greek city-states begin to form and the population grows. The Greeks trade their wine and olive oil around the Mediterranean.

432 BCE
The Parthenon is completed
Ruled by Pericles, the city of Athens completes the rebuilding of the temple of the Parthenon. It becomes a symbol of Athens' power and Greek culture.

323 BCE
The death of Alexander the Great
Alexander dies young after building a huge empire around the Mediterranean and in western Asia. Greek culture is spread all over these areas.

LIVING IN ANCIENT GREECE

Be like an ancient Greek and set out on a journey of discovery. For over a thousand years, the ancient Greeks left their homes to travel far and wide around the Mediterranean. They traded with other people and set up new ports and towns. They created a Greek-speaking world whose ideas are still important today – including those about art, science, medicine and politics. On our journey, we will meet the children and young people of ancient Greece: Timarete, a young woman artist, and Cosimo, a trainee bard. There's Lysander, who wants to be an actor, and Cassie, who wants to get to vote. Sebastian is an oarsman who dreams of owning a market stall, while Agnodike has become a female doctor, against the odds. Alongside them, you'll meet children working on the farm, in the pottery workshop and at the barber's shop. You'll hear the clash of weapons, gossip at the market, music lessons and philosophical debate. You'll even watch the ancient Olympics! Life is never quiet in ancient Greece...

THE YOUNG PRIESTESS

The Minoan civilisation grew up on the island of Crete more than a thousand years before ancient Greece began. The Minoans were not Greeks but they influenced later Greek art and culture.

Mysterious Minoans
We don't know what the Minoans called themselves. Our name for them comes from the legend of King Minos of Crete in Greek mythology.

Hello, I'm Rhea! I'm learning to be a priestess. I help take care of the Great Goddess at the temple.

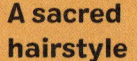
RHEA

A sacred hairstyle
Priestesses had their long hair tied in a knot at the back of their necks, like the goddess they worshipped. They wore bright clothes and heavy make up.

Bull leaping
The Minoans left many images of young people leaping over bulls. These acrobatic displays were probably part of religious festivals.

In Minoan art women were shown with lighter skins than men. Here you can see Rhea and another priestess helping a young man to somersault over a bull.

I've got the bull by the horns!

Great palaces

The Minoans built at least five great palaces on Crete. Minoan rulers governed their people from these complexes, which held temples, archive rooms (like libraries) and workshops.

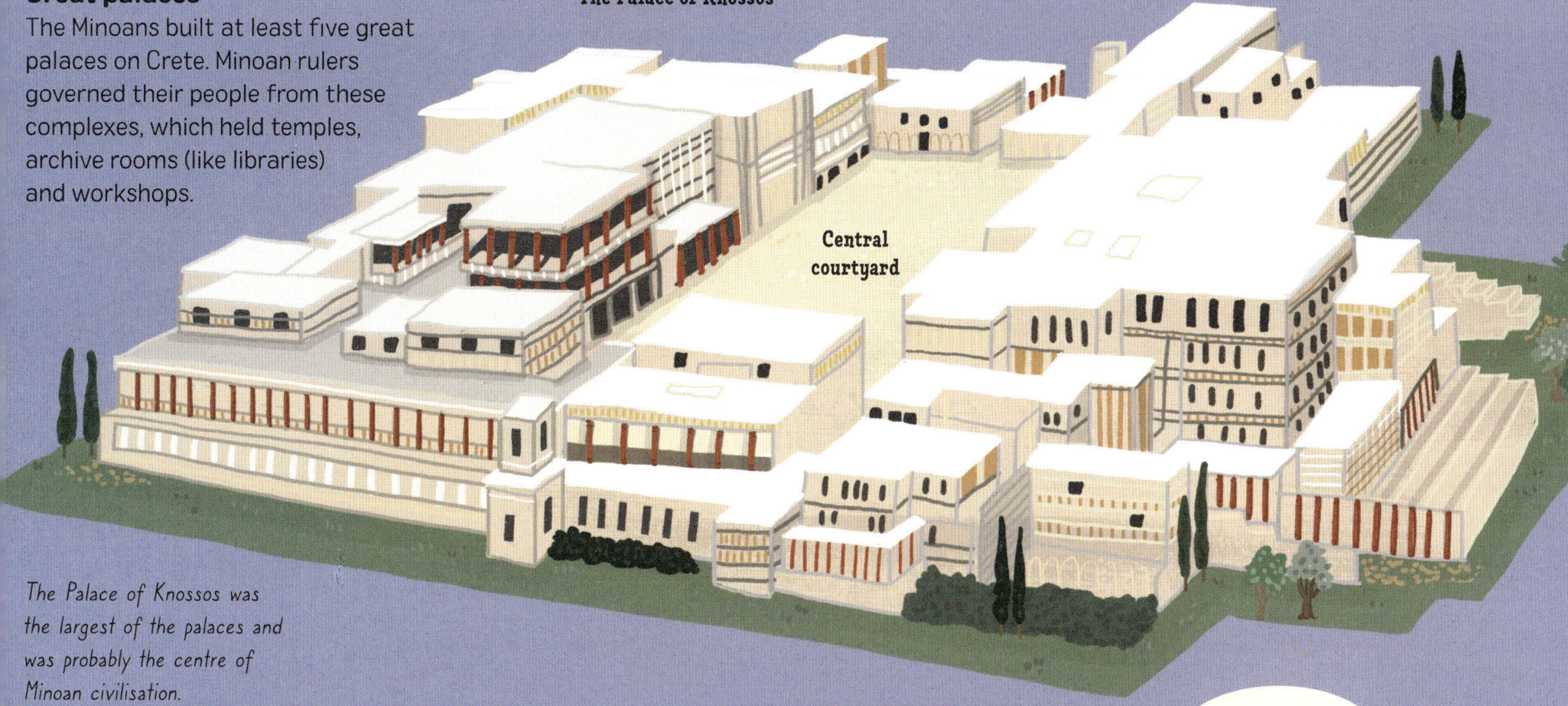

The Palace of Knossos

Central courtyard

The Palace of Knossos was the largest of the palaces and was probably the centre of Minoan civilisation.

The Minoans made tiny statues of a goddess or priestess holding snakes. She is known as the Snake Goddess.

Minoan religion
The central god in Minoan religion was a female "mother goddess". Her statue was kept in temples and was cared for by a number of priestesses. There are many frescoes (wall paintings) and other images of Minoan religious ceremonies. Often they seem to be led by goddesses and priestesses.

Minoan art
The walls of Minoan palaces were decorated with beautiful frescoes of animals and people. These tells us a lot about the Minoans and how they lived.

A fresco is a wall painting made by applying fresh plaster to a wall and painting it while it is still wet. It is then left to dry. Frescoes can last for many centuries.

"I paint the best dolphins!"

WRITING THAT NO ONE CAN READ
The Minoans wrote on clay tablets in a writing system we call Linear A, but no one today has worked out how to read it. It was used until about 1450 BCE. Another writing system, called Linear B, replaced it. Linear B was used by the Mycenaeans of Greece, who were greatly influenced by the Minoans. Experts can read Linear B, because it is based on the Greek language.

An example of Minoan writing. Only a few of the symbols have been decoded.

Greek colonies

The Greeks left Greece for many different reasons, including overcrowding, famine and war. But the main reason they went to new places was to grow their trade and to make their home cities richer. We call these settlements colonies. The red areas on this map show the areas that were part of the Greek world at this time.

Visiting the oracle

The Greeks worshipped many gods and goddesses. Apollo was one of the most important. Before setting out to found a new colony, the expedition leaders went to his temple at Delphi to see its high priestess. She was known as the Oracle of Delphi. She told them if their journey would be successful.

The Oracle sat on a tall three-legged stool as she made predictions about the future.

> Hello, I'm Galen! We live in Massalia, in France.

The colony of Massalia in what is now France became an important port and still is today. It is now called Marseille.

GALEN

FRANCE
MASSALIA
EMPORIAE
ITALY
ALALIA
NEAPOLIS
SPAIN
SARDINIA
HEMEROSCOPIUM
MEDITERRANEAN SEA
HIMERA
SICILY
SYRAC*
NORTH AFRICA

THE GREEK WORLD

From around 800 BCE, as the population grew, groups of Greeks left their homeland to settle around the Mediterranean and the Black Sea. As a result there were Greek-speaking children growing up all around these areas. Many kept in contact with their Greek roots, but over time they joined the local culture.

The Phoenicians were expert sailors. They came from the city of Tyre on the Eastern Mediterranean.

The Phoenicians

The Greeks competed with the Phoenicians, another great nation of trading peoples. The Phoenicians controlled most of the coast of North Africa and southern Spain.

AGRICULTURE AND FOOD

DOROTHEA   ANASTASIA

NANNY GOAT

Hello! We are twins. I'm Anastasia and this is Dorothea. We live in Sparta. Dad's always away so we help our mum to run the farm.

A FARMING FAMILY

Most ancient Greeks lived with their families on the land and made a living as farmers. They produced most of their own food and clothing, but exchanged some things they couldn't make themselves.

Farm animals
Sheep and goats were the most common farm animals as they were best suited to the dry, stony ground. They were kept for their milk and wool, while pigs and chickens were raised for meat and eggs. Cows gave milk and oxen were used for pulling ploughs.

Farming in Sparta
Women did farm work all over Greece, but in Sparta they often ran the farms and households. Spartan men were almost always away fighting in wars, often against other Greek cities.

The twins are very happy because their favourite nanny goat has just had triplets!

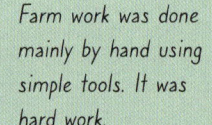

Farm work was done mainly by hand using simple tools. It was hard work.

Crops
Barley was the most common crop. Its grain was ground into flour for making bread and gruel (a sort of porridge). Some farmers planted wheat but it did not grow well in Greece's dry soil, so it was mostly brought in from the colonies. Farmers also grew broad beans, chickpeas and lentils.

Farmers ploughed the fields and planted wheat and barley in October. The crops grew in the winter and spring, when the most rain fell. Harvest time was in May or June.

Wine and olive oil

Olives and grapes were important crops. Some olives were preserved to be eaten with meals, but most of them were made into oil. Grapes were grown all over Greece. At harvest time, people ate a few bunches fresh and dried some in the sun to eat as raisins, but most grapes were made into wine.

The twins use long sticks to shake the ripe olives out of the trees.

The girls have fun stamping the grapes in a trough to make wine.

FOOD

The Greeks had a simple, healthy diet based on grains, vegetables, fruit, fish, beans, cheese and olive oil. Most families grew all the food they needed on their small farms.

The Greeks ate vegetables such as cucumbers, onions and garlic.

They also ate fruit and nuts, such as apples, figs, pomegranates and almonds.

Trade and barter

If the farmers grew more food than they could eat, they would take it to sell or trade in the local market. They might exchange, or barter, their produce for other things they needed, such as pottery or other types of food.

Ancient Greeks matured the cheese by hanging it from branches in the sun, using cloth bags.

THE ORIGINS OF CHEESE

The Greeks made and ate cheese, including a soft, white cheese very like feta. At the end of the 8th century BCE, the ancient Greek poet Homer described a one-eyed monster making cheese in his epic poem *The Odyssey* (see page 18).

Feta is made from sheep or goats milk, or sometimes the two combined.

"Who wants some lovely ripe fruit?"

"Delicious garlic! Two for a jug!"

THE YOUNG BARD

The stories about Greek gods, goddesses and heroes that we still read today date back thousands of years. Some came from the Minoans via the early Mycenaean Greeks, others from places the Greeks colonised. These myths were passed down the generations by wandering storytellers called bards.

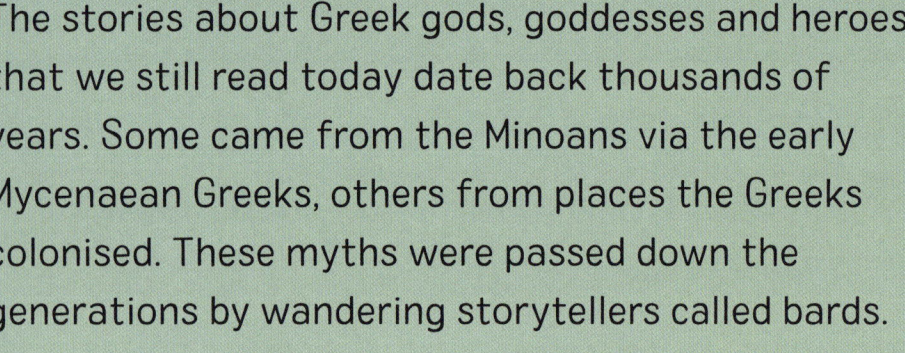

COSIMO

Hi, I'm Cosimo! I'm ten and I'm learning to be a bard. I have to know all the myths and legends by heart. It's a lot to remember!

Life of a bard
Bards were entertainers who travelled from village to village bringing news and telling stories. They performed at religious feasts, celebrations and village festivals.

Homer
The Iliad and *The Odyssey* are two epic* poems by Homer. They tell the myth of the Trojan War and the adventures of Odysseus, a Greek king, on his way home from the war. Homer lived in the 8th century BCE before writing was widespread so his poems were kept alive by bards.

HOMER

*An epic is a very long poem that tells the story of a hero who does great things or goes on a long journey.

ICARUS

One myth tells how the boy Icarus flew with wings made of feathers and wax. But he went too close to the sun and the wax melted...

Ha! He thought he was so clever.

So many stories!
Greek mythology is so rich because the stories were invented by different people over many centuries. They deal with subjects like the creation of life, the seasons, heroes and gods.

Bards usually played the lyre or a flute to accompany their stories.

THE OLYMPIANS

The Greeks believed that twelve of their most important gods and goddesses lived on Mount Olympus, Greece's highest mountain. These were the Olympians. Some myths include the goddess Hestia as the twelfth Olympian, while others have the god Dionysus. We show both here.

Zeus, god of the sky and thunder, the chief god.

Poseidon, god of the seas.

Hera, goddess of women and childbirth, Zeus's wife.

Athena, goddess of wisdom.

Demeter, goddess of the harvest.

Apollo, god of healing, music, poetry and prophecy.

Artemis, goddess of wild animals and hunting.

Ares, god of war and courage.

Aphrodite, goddess of love, beauty and pleasure.

Hephaestus, god of blacksmiths, metalwork and crafts.

Hermes, messenger of the gods. God of travel, athletes, sports, mischief and trade.

Hestia, goddess of the hearth (a fireplace where people cooked) and home.

Dionysus, god of wine, fruit and the theatre.

Let's not forget **Hades,** god of the dead. But he lived in the underworld.

THE HOPLITE

Ancient Greece was not one big country but divided into city-states. These states often fought each other and neighbouring peoples. All Greek men were expected to fight. They were not full time soldiers, but farmers and craftsmen who trained to be ready to fight when needed.

Hi, I'm Atticus! I'm a hoplite, a foot soldier.

ATTICUS

The Mycenaeans placed golden death masks on the faces of their dead rulers to go with them to the spirit world. This one perhaps belonged Agamemnon, the Mycenaean king at the time of the Trojan War.

A tradition of warfare
Some of the first Greek warriors were the Mycenaeans, who ruled parts of Greece from 1700–1100 BCE. They built great palaces and traded around the Mediterranean. They also fought the Trojan War. We learn a lot about Greek ways of fighting from Homer's *Iliad*.

Hoplites were foot soldiers. They carried long spears and a shield called a "hoplon". They wore bronze breastplates and helmets.

The Trojan Horse
The Iliad includes the myth of the wooden horse. The Trojans took it into their city, thinking it was a gift from the Greeks. Instead, there were soldiers hidden inside. They came out at night and opened the city gates. The Greeks sacked Troy and won the war.

They fell for it! Let's open the gates.

Archaeologists have found Troy, the city of the Trojans, and shown that the Greeks once fought there.

Battle strategies
Homer's descriptions of battle often emphasise one-to-one combat or fights in small groups. But the Greeks also developed battle strategies that involved huge groups of hoplites fighting in formation.

The phalanx
Atticus would have been part of a phalanx, made up of row upon row of heavily armed hoplites. The front row pushed into the enemy army using their shields and with their spears out. As their row fell apart, the next one moved in.

Two armies march into one another in the phalanx formation. The piper at the centre may have helped set the speed the army marched at.

The tightly packed phalanx fell apart row by row. When his row broke, Atticus used his sword to fight.

ALEXANDER THE GREAT
Alexander (356–323 BCE) was King of Macedonia in northern Greece. He was a brilliant general, who used his skills and his armies to take control of all of Greece and beyond, creating one of the largest empires in history. This empire included Egypt and stretched as far as north-west India. He founded more than twenty cities, including Alexandria in Egypt. He died when he was only 32, but his conquests spread Greek culture far and wide and inspired future empire builders, such as the Romans.

Alexander was famous for his use of cavalry (soldiers on horseback) in his battles. His favourite horse was called Bucephalus.

The map shows Alexander's journey of conquest and the vast empire he ruled.

THE OARSMAN

As well as fighting on land, the Greeks developed ships to fight at sea too. From the 7th to 4th centuries BCE, they ruled the waves with their triremes – large battleships that needed lots of oarsman to row fast and ram them into the enemy.

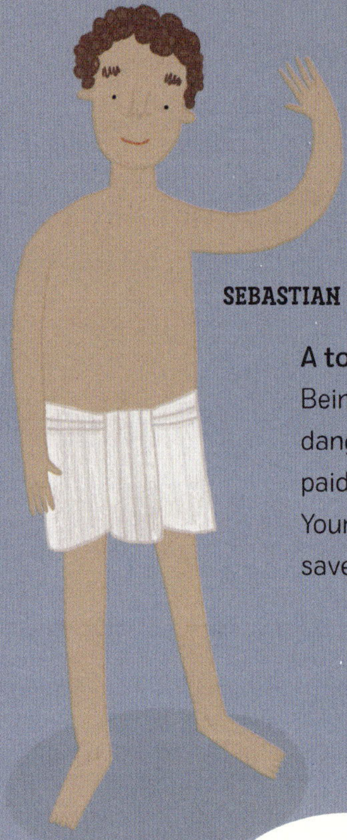

Triremes
Triremes were over 35 metres long and had three banks of oars. Each ship needed 180 oarsman. The Greeks used a huge fleet of triremes to defeat the Persian navy at the Battle of Salamis in 480 BCE.

Hello! I'm Sebastian. My family's poor. We can't afford a hoplite's armour so I've become an oarsman.

SEBASTIAN

A tough and dangerous life
Being an oarsman was a tough and dangerous life, but oarsmen were paid (1 drachma a day) and fed. Young men, like Sebastian, could save for their life in the future.

Sebastian sits just above the waterline, in the bottom of the three rows of oarsmen. He manages to keep rowing by dreaming of the market stall he will own one day.

Ugh! It's smelly! His feet are right in my face!

Altogether now! Stroke!

TYPES OF BATTLESHIPS

The triremes were the largest of the Greek battleships. They developed from smaller boats. The earliest, the pentecontor, had one row of 25 oars on each side. Next came the bireme, which the Greeks probably adapted from the Phoenicians. The largest biremes had two rows of 30 oars on each side, which needed 120 oarsmen.

Ramming the enemy
Before battle, ships lowered their masts then rammed into an enemy's ship. If this did not sink it, soldiers boarded to fight for control.

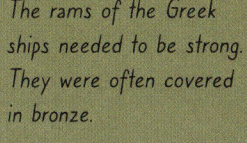

The rams of the Greek ships needed to be strong. They were often covered in bronze.

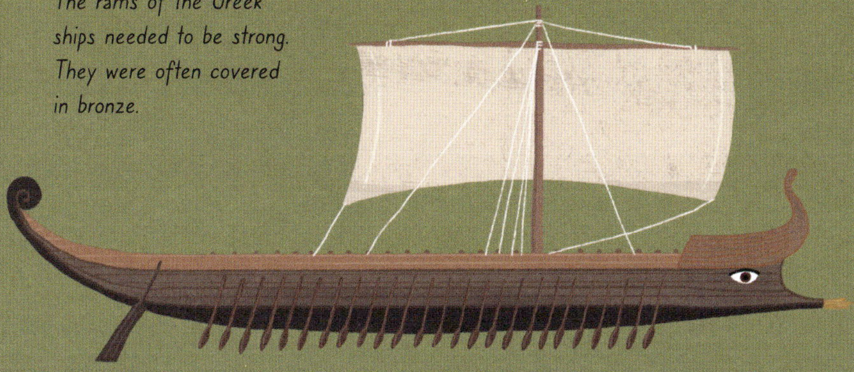

Penteconter

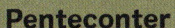

Bireme

"Get ready to ram!"

THE APPRENTICE POTTER

The Greeks used clay to make many types of pottery. There were pots and jars for storage and everyday use, but they also made beautiful painted vases, cups and jugs.

Hi, I'm Basil! I'm nine and I work in our family workshop. We make pots and fire them in the big kiln.

The potter's wheel
The potters dug up the clay they needed from the ground. They cleaned it thoroughly and kneaded it to make it smooth before they used it. Then they threw the clay on a wheel, shaping it in their hands as the wheel turned.

In the workshop
A pottery workshop was very busy. There were people preparing clay, throwing pots and then firing them in the kiln (baking them in a large oven). Younger workers like Basil might help turn the wheel, attach handles, load pots into the kiln or just clean up after everyone.

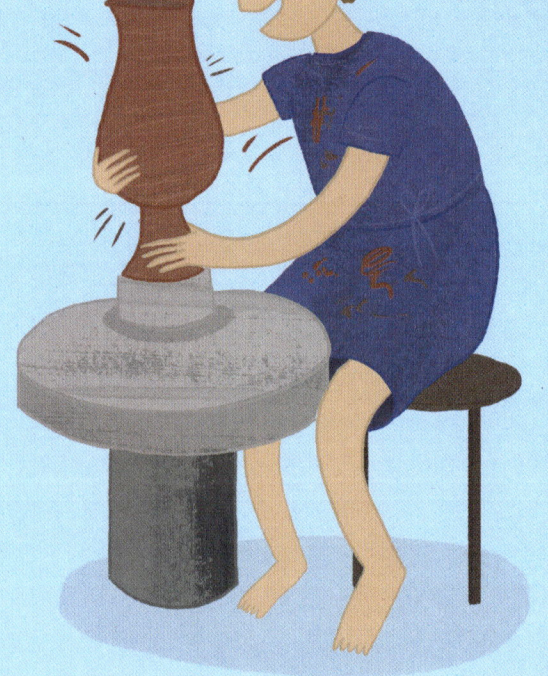

Basil's elder brother is expert on the wheel. He can turn the wheel with his knees but sometimes Basil helps.

Is this where the handles go?

Basil's father paints the pots. Pottery painters could become famous and people collected their work, like artists today.

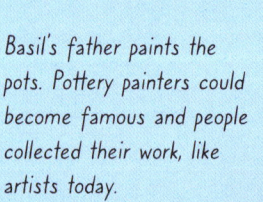

I'll paint a battle scene today. They always sell well.

Handles were stuck to pots using wet, runny clay. Basil is learning how to do this but he makes mistakes.

Decorating pots
Expert craftworkers painted the pots using a kind of coloured liquid clay called slip. They painted the areas they wanted to become black when the pot was fired. Some pots were decorated with geometric patterns. Others were decorated with scenes from myths and legends or daily life. These tell us a lot about what the Greeks thought and how they lived.

TYPES OF GREEK POTTERY

Pottery can last for a very long time, so archaeologists have found a lot of ancient Greek pottery. They name pots by their shapes and uses, and the style there were painted in. Black-figure painting picked out people in black. The later red-figure painting reversed this, with the paler figures on black backgrounds.

Black-figure painting

Red-figure painting

Amphora A large storage jar, particularly used for storing wine, olive oil and other liquids.

Krater Used to mix and serve wine with water.

Kylix Used as a drinking cup, particularly for wine.

Hydra Used as a jug for carrying water.

Oinoche Used as a jug for serving wine.

The kiln

The kiln was the oven where the pots were baked hard. Decorated pots would be fired three times as the different layers of decoration were put on. The kiln was buried partly underground and covered with a dome. This dome was rebuilt after each firing.

A hole at the top of the kiln let out fumes and may have helped the potter check on the firing.

Selling the pots

The finished pots were sold. Everyday pots were sold at local markets but the highest quality pots were traded all over the Greek world. The cities of Athens and Corinth were particularly famous for their pottery.

Basil's uncle has a stall in the local market. Basil likes to help out there sometimes, too.

WOMEN'S SPORT

Women were not allowed to compete at the Olympics and they could not come to watch. There were separate sporting events for women, including the Heraean Games, which were held in the Olympic Stadium every four years but at a different time.

The Heraean Games were dedicated to the goddess Hera, wife of Zeus.

Women winners

Even though they were banned, some women did win prizes at the Olympics due to a loophole in the rules. The owners and trainers of horses in the chariot racing and riding events won the prizes, not the riders or charioteers.

Kyniska of Sparta won victory wreaths on two occasions when her chariots won their races. She was their trainer. She knew how drive a chariot but could not take part in the race.

The Olympic Truce

At the time of the Olympic Games, a truce was called between any fighting city-states so people could travel safely to Olympia. They came from all over the Mediterranean.

The Sanctuary of Zeus

The Olympic Games were dedicated to Zeus, the chief god. They were held in his honour at Olympia. Here, the temple had a giant statue of Zeus. It was considered one of the Seven Wonders of the World.

A great meeting

Huge feasts were held throughout the Games. Cattle were sacrificed at the temple and then the meat was cooked and shared among the athletes and spectators.

"Hi, I'm Theo! I'm here at the Olympics with my dad. We walked for 10 days to get here!"

THEO'S DAD
THEO

THE OLYMPICS

The Olympic Games took place every four years from 776 BCE. All free Greek men and boys could compete or attend. The Games were a huge, five-day festival.

"I'm looking forward to the wrestling."

"I think the pankration is the best."

Wrestling To win at wrestling an athlete had to press his opponent's hip, shoulder or back to the ground three times. Biting was not allowed!

Long jump Some athletes held weights in their hands to increase the length of the jump. They threw them backwards as they landed.

Discus The throwing technique was similar to today's. At first the discus was made of stone then later of iron, lead or bronze.

Javelin The javelins were made of olive wood. Contestants had to throw them as far as possible.

PROGRAMME OF EVENTS

Pankration This fierce sport was a mix of wrestling and boxing. The only rules were no poking at eyes or noses and no biting.

Day 1 Athletes and organisers swearing-in ceremony. Prayers and sacrifices in the sanctuary of Zeus. Consultation of oracles. Speeches.
Day 2 Chariot and horse races, and the pentathlon (made up of five events).
Day 3 Procession to the Great Altar. Sacrifices. Public banquet.
Day 4 Wrestling, boxing and pankration. Running.
Day 5 Procession of winners to the Temple of Zeus to be crowned with garlands of wild olive.

Boxing The boxers wrapped their hands and wrists with leather straps. The winner had to knock his opponent out or force him to give up.

Running events There were several running contests over various distances. In one race, the contestants wore armour and carried shields!

WINNERS
There were no medals at the ancient Olympics. Judges chose a single winner for each competition and he was crowned with a wreath of olive leaves.

Equestrian events These included horse riding and chariot races. The winner was the owner of the chariot or horses, not the racers.

THE FISHMONGER

Life in Greek towns and cities was centred on an open space called the agora. It was a busy marketplace, but also where people came to meet friends, vote, discuss politics and hold religious ceremonies.

PHOEBE

Hi, I'm Phoebe! I'm 13 and I keep our family fish stall in the agora. My dad is a fisherman. My mum died when I was little.

A pop-up shoemaker's stall in the agora. The craftsman carefully measures his customer's foot.

Phoebe sells the fish her father catches. She works every day, chatting to other working women, servants and slaves who visit the agora. Wealthy Greek women were rarely seen outside the home.

Traders
The agora was home to many small family businesses like Phoebe's family fishmongers. Other stalls sold pottery, meats, vegetables, homemade cheese and wine, and cloth or clothing that women wove and sewed in their homes.

Craftspeople
There were small, dark workshops around the agora for craftsmen such as shoemakers and blacksmiths. They sold what they made from little shops at the workshop door. Craftsmen were not always highly valued in Greece, and many were foreigners or slaves.

A meeting place for all
The law courts and city government offices were all based in the agora in Athens, the centre of one of Greece's major city-states. Citizens also came there to talk about the issues of the day and to vote.

SLAVERY
There were many slaves in ancient Greece. They were often prisoners taken in war, kidnapped, or sold into slavery from far-off lands. There were different types of slavery. Many were their master's property and could be bought and sold like cattle. Others had more control over their lives.

Most slaves worked on farms. Others were employed in mines, digging out silver and gold for jewellery, and copper and tin to make bronze tools.

I wish I was a house slave!

It's hard work in the mines!

Wealthy families in Athens had at least three or four slaves for household chores.

THE CLUMSY CHORUS BOY

Most Greek cities had an outdoor theatre, called an amphitheatre, often built on the side of a hill in a clever way that meant the actors' voices could be heard high up by the audience.

Types of play
There were different types of play: comedies, tragedies and some that were mixes of both. Performances were linked to religion and the worship of the god Dionysus.

The actors
Only boys and men performed in plays. The actors playing the main parts were on a raised stage.

Hi, I'm Lysander. I want to be an actor. Today was my first time on stage and I messed it up so badly!

LYSANDER

A hoist

But if I am young, you should look to my merits, not to my years.

The stage

A man, though wise, should never be ashamed of learning more, and must unbend his mind.

Masks
Actors performed in masks. Each of the main actors' masks had a particular character but the chorus's masks were all the same.

GREEK PLAYWRIGHTS

Greek theatre dates back to the 6th century BCE. Some playwrights became very famous. Aeschylus (c. 525–456 BCE) was known as the "Father of Tragedy" for his powerful plays based on Greek myths and wars. Sophocles (c.497–406 BCE) and Euripides (c.480–406 BCE) were also famous for their tragedies. Their plays were written down and have survived until today. They are still often performed. The traditions of Western theatre began in ancient Greece.

The actors on these pages are reciting from "Antigone", a tragedy written by Sophocles.

AESCHYLUS

Boys like Lysander trained to be actors from a young age. When they were ready, they began performing as part of the chorus.

Plays were performed as part of huge festivals. A large amphitheatre could seat around 20,000 people in the audience.

"Nobody has a more sacred obligation to obey the law than those who make the law."

Lysander is so excited to be in the orchestra that he loses his footing during the first performance. Everyone laughs! They think it's part of the show.

"Bravo!"

The chorus
A group of actors called the chorus performed in a space in front of the stage called the orchestra. They commented on the action in the play.

"Behold! The mighty... Ooops!"

"Not many in today."

The orchestra

A WOMAN DOCTOR

In the early days, the ancient Greeks thought that good health was a gift from the gods and they treated illness with magic and rituals. But by 500 BCE, Greek doctors began to develop scientific methods to treat disease and stay healthy.

AGNODIKE

Hi, I'm Agnodike! I'm 18 and I want to be a doctor. Girl aren't allowed to study medicine, so I dress as a boy to go to class.

Ouch! Steady on. That hurts!

Agnodike's story
Agnodike was a real woman born in Athens in the 4th century BCE. She really wanted to be a doctor so she went to Alexandria to study medicine, dressing up as a boy. She graduated with flying colours and returned to Athens. She became so popular there that she was able to work openly as a women.

Most ancient Greek doctors were men. The few women that worked generally specialised in childbirth and women's health.

Surgery
Anesthetic wasn't invented until the 19th century CE, so surgery was very painful in ancient Greece. Even so, many Greek doctors were skilled surgeons. There were also dentists who would remove rotten teeth. They did not have fillings.

A good career
Greek doctors were famous for their knowledge and skills. Some became rich by treating wealthy and powerful people or working as city doctors paid by the government. Others were less well paid and they moved from town to town, setting up surgeries to treat people in each place.

Sports medicine
The Greeks believed that a healthy body was very important. They loved sport and most towns and cities had public gymnasiums where people went to train – and to relax.

Greek boys trained from an early age. We know less about girls exercising, except for in Sparta where girls worked out alongside their brothers.

THE FATHER OF MEDICINE

Hippocrates is the most famous Greek doctor and he is often referred to as the "Father of Medicine". He believed that sickness came from natural causes and was not a punishment from the gods. He told people that plenty of sleep, exercise and a healthy diet were essential for good health.

Hippocrates was born on the island of Kos in about 460 BCE. Some say that he lived for well over 100 years; others say he died at the age of 85 or 90.

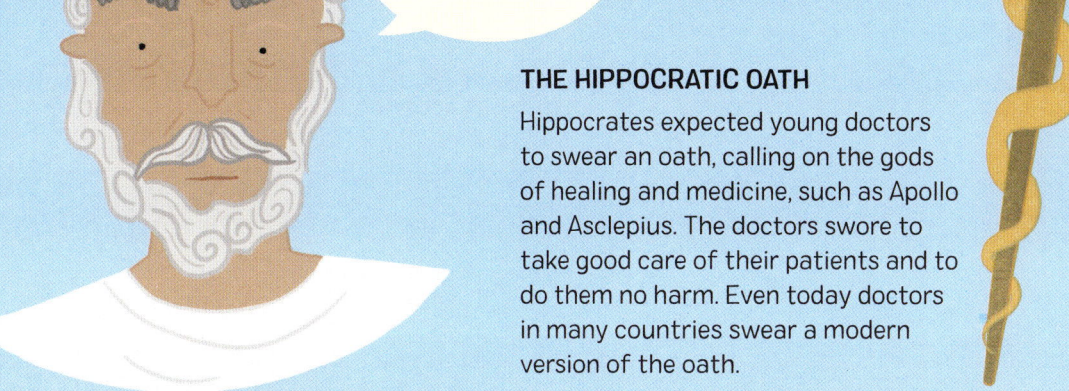

I swear by Apollo and by Asclepius...

HIPPOCRATES

The Rod of Asclepius

The rod of Asclepius has become a symbol of medicine and is still widely used today.

THE HIPPOCRATIC OATH

Hippocrates expected young doctors to swear an oath, calling on the gods of healing and medicine, such as Apollo and Asclepius. The doctors swore to take good care of their patients and to do them no harm. Even today doctors in many countries swear a modern version of the oath.

Wash your hands. Then I'll taste your earwax.

A 3rd-century BCE doctor called Theophrastus used a medicine based on cinnamon to treat infected war wounds. It is now known that cinnamon kills germs.

Sickness and remedies

The Greeks believed that the human body had four "humours" — blood, phlegm, yellow bile and black bile — and that disease was caused if these four got out of balance. They used herbs, foods and diet to cure illness, as well as clays, minerals and wine.

Although they didn't know about germs, the Greeks knew that cleanliness was essential for good health.

Asclepius, God of Medicine

According to Greek legend, the centaur Chiron invented medicine to heal himself after he was wounded by Hercules. Chiron taught his medical skills to a boy called Asclepius, who then became the god of medicine.

ASCLEPIUS

CHIRON

A centaur is a creature in Greek mythology who has the upper body of a man and the lower limbs of a horse.

Some very odd cures!

The Greeks made big advances in medicine but they still had some odd ideas and practices. For example, a doctor might nibble some of your earwax or lick your vomit to help diagnose your illness! If you had a rash, he might smear your skin with crocodile dung to help clear it up.

PHILOSOPHERS, POETS AND HISTORIANS

Here are three of the most famous thinkers.

Socrates (c. 470–399 BCE) is known as "the father of Western philosophy". He wrote nothing down. We know about him from people he taught, such as Plato (c. 427–347 BCE).

Sappho (c. 620–570 BCE) was a poet from the Greek island of Lesbos. She is known for lyric poetry, which was sung to music, often played on a lyre.

Herodotus (c. 484–425 BCE) was a historian. He wrote about the Greek wars with Persia. He is known as the "Father of History".

LEON GOES TO SCHOOL

Wealthy families sent their sons to school when they were about seven years old. Boys had to learn to be soldiers as well as poets and politicians. Physical education was considered as important as skills such as reading and writing.

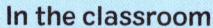
LEON

Abacus

Hi, I'm Leon! I'm eight and I go to school each day in Athens. I'm learning how to read and write — and to wrestle.

In the classroom
Boys learnt to read from scrolls (there were no books) and to write on wax tablets, melting the wax to use it again. There were maths lessons, sometimes using an abacus to work things out. They also learnt poetry by heart.

A schoolboy's day
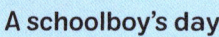
Classes were small and there was just one teacher. In the afternoon the boys had their physical education, which included wrestling.

Boys are taught music. Leon is learning the lyre, as well as how to sing and dance with the other boys.

Learning how to argue

Some boys left school at 14, but others went on to university-like academies. Here they learnt how to speak in public, argue and debate. They studied ideas through a way of thinking called philosophy.

Academy students might go on to become philosophers, historians, poets, playwrights and scientists.

"Ideas are the source of all things."

"As the philosopher Plato always says!"

Philosophers discussed ideas through asking and answering questions, a method made popular by Socrates.

A woman philosopher

Aspasia (c. 470-428 BCE) was one of few women linked with philosophy in ancient Greece. She is said to have debated with philosophers such as Socrates and to have started an academy for women.

SOCRATES

"Here's another way of looking at it."

ASPASIA

SCIENCE AND MATHS

The Greeks saw these as part of philosophy. Here are three more thinkers in these areas.

Archimedes (c. 287–212 BCE) made breakthroughs in maths, physics and astronomy. He was also an inventor.

Pythagoras (c. 570–495 BCE) was famous for maths, in particular geometry. He is credited with the Pythagoras Theorem we still learn today.

Aristarchus (c. 310–230 BCE) was the first astronomer to suggest that the Earth moved around the Sun.

ZOE STAYS AT HOME

Greek homes were run by the women and girls who lived there. They were allowed less freedom than the men and boys of the household, who came and went as they pleased. Few girls were taught to read or write and, if they were, their lessons took place at home.

ZOE

ZOE'S PET CAT DENIS

Hi, I'm Zoe! I am 11. I don't go to school. I stay home but I do study maths and letters. My mum also teaches me how to take care of our home.

Zoe is lucky because her family thinks she should have a good education. She has two tutors: one teaches her maths and about trade; the other how to read and write.

Educating girls
It was usually wealthier girls who were given a formal education, but not at school. Their mothers taught them how to run a large house and private tutors taught them to read and write. Some girls also studied maths and philosophy.

Music lessons
Almost all girls learnt to sing, dance or make music in some way so they could take part in religious events, such as weddings and funerals. The poetry they sang also taught them myths and legends.

I like Sappho's lyrics best.

Two afternoons a week Zoe and her friend have music lessons and practice sessions. They are learning to play the flute and the harp.

Kitchen

Gynaikon (women's room)

Andron (men's room)

Fun and games

Children did not spend all their time learning. They had time to play with their family and friends. They had toys and board games. They also had pets.

Zoe and her friend are playing knuckle bones, a game like jacks. They see how many bones they can pick up at a time.

Greek homes

Most Greek homes were made of mud bricks and wood. The windows did not have glass, so they were generally small and high up on the walls. They had to be repaired often as the walls could wear away. Wealthier families had houses made of stone which lasted longer.

The andron was a room for the men of the house. Here they could relax and meet with male friends.

Comfortable homes

The stone houses of richer families like Zoe's were large and comfortable. Like most homes, they were built around a central courtyard which had a well for water. There were sometimes religious shrines in the courtyard, as well as farmyard animals.

THE WOMEN'S ROOM

Large houses had a special room, called the gynaikon, set aside for the women of the household. Here they could work on spinning and weaving cloth and making clothes for the family. They could also look after their children and meet with their female friends.

Zoe learns how to use a spindle to prepare the wool thread for weaving.

Spinning and weaving

Women and girls made woollen cloth in the home – and all the family clothes. They would spin the wool into thread using a spindle and then weave it into cloth on the loom.

Zoe watches her mother set up the loom. Learning to spin and weave was an important part of a girl's education.

THE GOSSIPY BARBER'S SHOP

Hi, I'm Mikkos! I'm ten. I'm going to be a barber like my dad, Simo.

MIKKOS

Hi, I'm Cassie! I'm nine and I help out in our barber shop, too.

CASSIE

The Greeks loved to talk about politics, especially in democratic Athens where all citizens (men only) had a vote. Wherever Athenians gathered, like Simo's barber shop, there was sure to be lots of gossip and rowdy political discussion. Everyone had an opinion!

Taxes are too high!

I would like to vote too! Why can't women vote?

We need better schools!

Citizenship
About a quarter of the people living in Athens were citizens. Only they could own property, take part in festivals and vote. Women, foreigners, slaves and boys under 18 could not be citizens.

FORMS OF GOVERNMENT
There were four main forms of government in Greece. Very simply, these were:
Democracy - rule by the people (male citizens).
Monarchy - rule by an individual (a king) who had inherited his power.
Oligarchy - rule by a small group of individuals.
Tyranny - rule by an individual who had seized power against the law.

Greek ideas of democracy have influenced politics to this day – although now far more people, including women, are citizens and are able to vote. The best known Greek democracy was found in Athens.

The owl was a symbol of wisdom and the goddess Athena. It became an emblem of Athens and was shown on its coins.

Greek city-states

Ancient Greece was not a single, united country. It was made up of hundreds of independent city-states. Each one had its own form of government. Sparta, for example, was a monarchy, ruled by two kings and a council of elders. Meanwhile in Athens all adult male citizens had the right to vote. This was an early form of democracy.

This map shows how Greece was divided in 431 BCE. The city-states and the areas they controlled changed over time. They were often at war with each other and became allies (joined together) to fight.

- ATHENS AND ITS ALLIES: YELLOW
- SPARTA AND ITS ALLIES: RED
- NEUTRAL CITY-STATES: BLUE
- KINGDOM OF MACEDONIA: GREEN

Voting in a democracy

Athenian citizens came together to vote on laws, elect their leaders and decide on important matters, such as whether to go to war. People made speeches and a vote was taken by a show of hands.

These small, bronze discs were used for voting in Athens after a secret ballot was introduced, so no one could see how you voted.

Vote for war against Sparta!

He gets my vote!

Greek women got the vote in 1952, about 2,500 years after I asked!

PERICLES

A great leader

Pericles (c. 495–429 BCE) was a leader of Athens, voted into power by its citizens. He was also a great general (which is why he wears a helmet). He helped make Athens the most powerful of the Greek city-states and a centre of learning and the arts.

THE YOUNG PAINTER

The ancient Greeks created beautiful art and buildings. Only fragments of paintings, mainly frescoes, have survived, but we know about them and their creators from writers of the time and later historians. A very few artists were women, such as Timarete.

Hi, I'm called Timarete. My dad taught me to paint in his studio. Now I've become quite a famous artist.

TIMARETE

Timarete lived in the 5th century BCE. Her father, Micon, was known for his paintings of battles. Her best-known painting was of the goddess Diana.

Paintings everywhere
The Greeks had paintings on wooden panels in their houses and temples. Like the Minoans, the Greeks painted frescoes on their walls and ceilings.

This diver was painted on the ceiling of a tomb in the 5th century BCE. The tomb is near to an ancient Greek settlement in Italy.

Surprise!

This gorgon – a snake-headed monster – is found at the bottom a drinking cup painted around 520 BCE.

A later bronze statue of a warrior.

An early stone kore (a female figure).

Sculptures
The Greeks made sculptures, particularly of the human body, carved from stone or cast in bronze. Ones from earlier periods were very stylised but later they became more lifelike. Statues were painted bright colours but these wore away over time.

Vase painting
Greek vase painting was another important art (see page 25). Greek styles of vase painting changed over the centuries. As in their sculpture, the painted figures became more realistic. This art was useful as well as beautiful.

THOLOS TEMPLE

DORIC TEMPLE

The tops of temples were decorated with beautifully carved and painted friezes and statues.

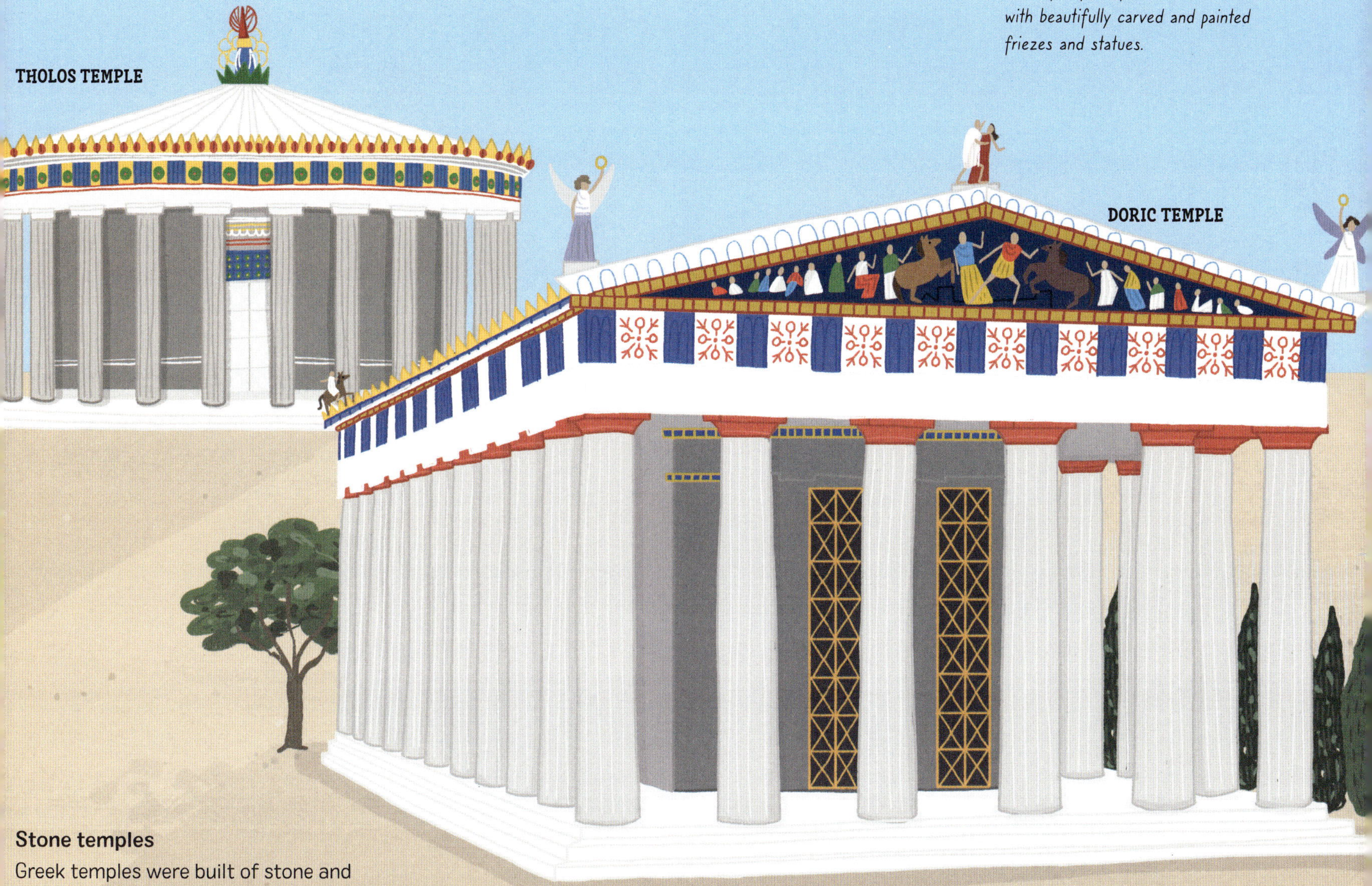

Stone temples

Greek temples were built of stone and painted in bright colours. They were centres of religion, with statues of Greek gods and goddesses inside them. It took a lot of time and money to build a temple. They showed off a city's wealth and power. Greek temple design still influences architecture today.

Most temples were rectangular, and often surrounded by columns, although these could just be along the front. A few temples were circular.

DORIC   IONIC   CORINTHIAN

GREEK COLUMNS

Greek temples are grouped by their shape but also the style of their columns. There were three main styles of columns, depending on their capitals (tops) and bases.

Doric - the earliest design with a simple capital and shallow base.
Ionic - known for its spiral circle designs, like a shell, on the capitals. It has a base of piled discs.
Corinthian - the last and most elaborate design with capitals carved in the shapes of leaves and flowers and elegant, layered bases.

QUIZ TIME!

Let's check and see how much you learned! Keep a record of your answers (on some paper or your phone) and check the quiz answers to see if you were right. They are on page 44, just below the index.

1. Beginning in about 800 BCE the ancient Greeks established many colonies all around the Mediterranean and Black Seas.

○ TRUE
○ FALSE

2. The Minoans are famous for:

A. Building large palaces on Crete
B. Their bull-leaping rituals
C. The snake goddess
D. All of the above

3. Greek women never did any farm work.

○ TRUE
○ FALSE

4. The ancient Greeks consulted the Oracle at Delphi before setting out to found a colony. Why did they do this?

A. They wanted to know the weather
B. They wanted to know if they would succeed
C. They wanted Apollo to help them find a boat
D. None of the above

5. Which of the following farm animals did the ancient Greeks keep?

A. Sheep
B. Goats
C. Hens
D. Pigs and cows
E. All of the above

6. By the age of 32, Alexander the Great forged an empire that was the largest the ancient world had ever seen.

○ TRUE   ○ FALSE

7. The largest Greek warship was called a trireme.

8. Hoplites were foot soldiers. They were named for the shields they carried, which were called "hoplons".

○ TRUE   ○ FALSE

○ TRUE   ○ FALSE

9. What was the name of Alexander the Great's beloved horse?

A. Bucephalus
B. Arnold
C. Marina
D. Byron

10. Religion in ancient Greece. Which of the following statements is true?

A. They only believed in one god
B. They had many myths about their gods and goddesses
C. The people who recounted the myths in ancient Greece were called bards
D. Bards would play the piano when they told their stories

11. The ancient Greeks made pottery vessels and painted scenes on them. What did the scenes painted on the pots show?

A. Scenes of daily life
B. Details from myths and legends
C. Geometric shapes and patterns
D. All of the above

12. What was the name of the famous temple that stood above the agora in ancient Athens (and still stands today)?

A. The Pantheon
B. The Parthenon
C. Stonehenge
D. The Temple of Apollo

13. Greek boys and girls had plenty of books to study from.

○ TRUE
○ FALSE

14. Both men and women were allowed to compete at the ancient Olympic Games.

○ TRUE   ○ FALSE

15. How many types of government were there in ancient Greece?

A. Four
B. None
C. Six
D. There were no forms of government

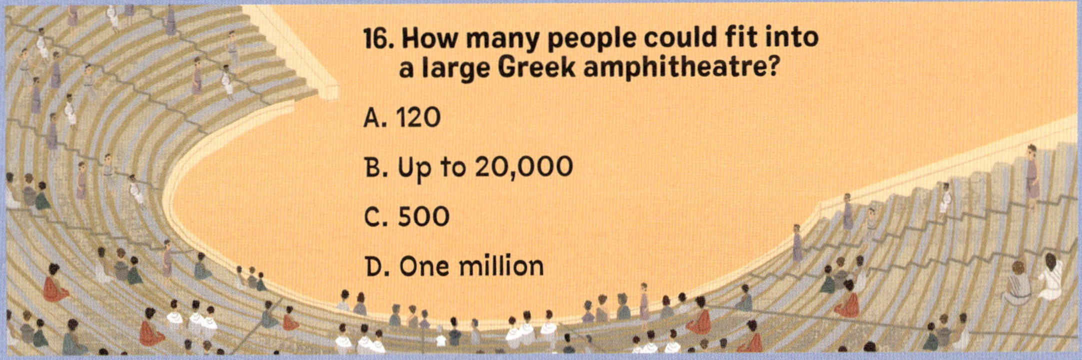

16. How many people could fit into a large Greek amphitheatre?

A. 120
B. Up to 20,000
C. 500
D. One million

17. Ancient Greek temples were painted in bright colours.

○ TRUE   ○ FALSE

18. All adults in ancient Athens were allowed to vote, including men, women, slaves and foreigners.

○ TRUE   ○ FALSE

19. What was a gynaikon?

A. A room in a large house reserved for men
B. The kitchen in a large townhouse
C. A room in a large house reserved for women
D. A type of musical instrument

20. Who was Hippocrates? Why was he famous?

A. He was a mathematician
B. He was a doctor and is known as the "Father of Medicine"
C. He was a great general
D. He was a Roman Emperor

INDEX

A
Actors 30-31
Alexander the Great 10, 21
Art 12-13, 24, 40
Athens 10, 25, 28-29, 32, 38-39

C
City-states 10, 20, 39
Clothes 12, 28, 37
Colonies 14-15
Crafts 24, 28
Crete 10, 12
Crops 16-17

D
Democracy 38-39

F
Farming 16-17
Festivals 12, 18, 26, 31
Fish 17, 28-29
Food 16-17, 28-29

G
Gods and goddesses 12-13, 14-15, 18, 26, 29, 33, 38

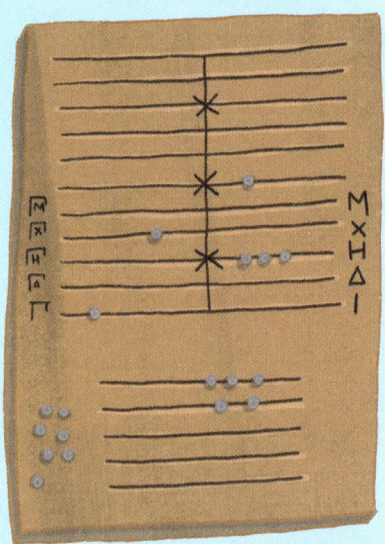

H
Health 32-33
Houses 36-37

M
Markets 17, 25, 28-29
Medicine 32-33
Minoans 10, 12-13
Music 34, 36
Mycenaeans 10, 13, 20
Myths 18

O
Olympic Games 26-27
Oracle of Delphi 14

P
Painting 12-13, 24-25, 40-41
Palaces 12-13
Philosophy 34-35
Plays 30-31
Poems and poets 17, 18, 34-35, 36
Politics 28-29, 38
Pottery 24-25
Priests and priestesses 12-13, 14

R
Religion 12, 19, 30, 41

S
Schools 34-35
Science 35
Ships 22-23
Slavery 28
Sparta 16, 32, 39
Sport 26-27, 32

T
Temples 10, 14-15, 26, 29, 41
Theatre 30-31
Timeline 10
Trade 10, 14, 17, 28-29,
Trojans 10, 18, 20

W
Wars 10, 16, 20-21, 39
Weapons 20-21
Weaving 37
Women 12, 16, 26, 28, 32, 35, 36-37, 40
Writing 10, 13, 34, 36

ANSWERS TO THE QUIZ
(pages 42-43)

1	True	8	True	15	A
2	D	9	A	16	B
3	False	10	B, C	17	True
4	B	11	D	18	False
5	E	12	B	19	C
6	True	13	False	20	B
7	True	14	False